MOMS

IN TOUCH
INTERNATIONAL

TM

*Mothers Meeting to Pray
for Their Children
& Schools*

by Fern Nichols

Scripture references are taken from the
Amplified Translation of the Bible
unless otherwise noted.

Amplified New Testament
© The Lockman Foundation, 1954, 1958
Used by permission.

Moms In Touch International
P.O. Box 1120
Poway, California 92074-1120
619-486-4065

Table of Contents

Introduction

In the fall of 1984, while our family was living in Abbotsford, British Columbia, the two oldest of our four children were entering junior high school. I found myself with a heart heavy and burdened with concern for the new world they would be entering. They would be facing their greatest test in resisting immoral values, vulgar language and peer pressure. My heart cried out to the Lord asking Him to protect them, and enable them to see clearly the difference between right and wrong, and to make good decisions.

The burden to intercede for my boys was so overwhelming that I knew I could not bear it alone. I asked God to give me another mom who felt the same burden and who would be willing to pray with me concerning our children and their schools. God heard the cry of my heart and led me to phone another mom who voiced her agreement as I shared my burden. We also thought of a few other moms we believed would want to pray. We called them and began meeting the following week for prayer.

This was the beginning of what is now known as Moms In Touch International—moms in touch with God, their children, their school, and one another through prayer. As moms began sharing what God had been doing in their lives, and in the lives of their children because of prayer, other groups began to spring up all over British Columbia. There were groups formed from the elementary through the high school levels. The initial material in this booklet was formulated during that year. What a thrill to see God's plan unfold!

The summer of 1985 brought a change to our family as we moved from Abbotsford to Poway, California. I soon discovered that God had given me still greater opportunities for carrying on the work that began in Canada. I prayed that God would raise up moms who were willing to "stand in the gap" for their children.

God has been faithful to send moms who would pray. There are now Moms In Touch International groups across America, as well as in other countries. Because moms were asking for guidelines on how to pray more effectively and how to begin a Moms In Touch group, we created this booklet.

I would like to acknowledge Sondra Ball, who has helped me put together this material. Her encouragement, suggestions, time, friendship, and loving support have been specific answers to my prayers.

It is my hope that God will raise up moms to intercede for every school across our nation and around the world. What a thrilling thought to consider two or more moms gathered together every week in prayer for their children and their schools.

Let me challenge you to be involved in your child's life through prayer. See what God can do for your children and their schools when you are faithful to pray on a regular basis.

Believing in the power of prayer,

Fern Nichols

Fern Nichols

MILLER

4

Personal Testimony

I would like to take a moment to share with you how God has worked in my personal life on the matter of prayer. Being asked to speak at a prayer retreat several years ago brought about some serious evaluation of my prayer life. Listening to several tapes on prayer by Ron Dunn helped me greatly. I also read many wonderful books on prayer, but I knew within my heart that listening to discussions about prayer, talking about prayer, or reading about prayer didn't make up for my lack of actually praying.

It seemed I was always praying "on the run." My prayer time was hit and miss. God, in His grace, allowed me to see that my priorities were not right. I was "busy," productive in many wonderful things, but I wasn't doing the best thing—spending consistent prayer time with God.

I believe that Satan has us thinking that being spiritual means being productive. He doesn't want us to cross over the invisible line into powerful intercessory prayer. If he can keep us thinking that being on the productive side of the line is doing great things for God, then we will secure few blessings for our family, schools, community, and nation. But if we recognize the line and cross over it to be intercessors, God will move heaven and earth to answer our prayers, and we will begin to see great victories and Satan's defeat. Satan trembles when he sees the weakest saint on his knees, for he knows he has no power against our prayers. Let me share with you a list of what I asked God to do in my life in this matter of prayer.

1. That I would be a woman of prayer.
2. That I would gain a vision for the power of prayer.
3. That I would seek to become an intercessor.

4. That I would begin to practice aggressive praying, taking the initiative to pray with others as a way of life.
5. That I would learn to pray through the scriptures.
6. That I might pray without ceasing.
7. That I would be able to communicate to others what God is teaching me in prayer.

If the Holy Spirit is speaking to your heart as you read this list, stop right now, heed His voice, and pray.

The ministry of prayer is one of the highest callings a Christian can have. Right now, Jesus is seated at the right hand of God interceding for you.

What is Moms In Touch?

- Two or more moms who meet for one hour each week to pray for their children, their schools, their teachers, and administrators.
- Mothers, grandmothers, or anyone who is willing to pray for a specific child and school.
- Moms who believe that prayer makes a difference!

Starting a Moms In Touch Group

- Pray that God brings you another mom who will be willing to meet with you each week for prayer. In faith, ask a mom to meet with you to pray for your child and his/her school.
- Make a list of prospective moms and ask them to join your prayer time.
- Follow the Moms In Touch International (MITI) guidelines and format for prayer time.
- Make sure you are controlled by the Holy Spirit. Trust God for answers to prayer, focus on Him, and expect great things to happen.

Purpose

- To stand in the gap for our children through prayer
- To pray that our children will receive Jesus as Lord and Savior, then stand boldly in their faith
- To pray for teachers and staff
- To pray that teachers, administrative staff, and students would come to faith in Jesus Christ
- To provide support and encouragement to moms who carry heavy burdens for their children
- To pray that our schools may be directed by biblical values and high moral standards
- To be an encouragement and a positive support to our schools

Moms In Touch International is not a lobbying group, regardless of how worthy the cause. Participation in outside political and social issues must be done solely on an individual basis. Under no circumstances should the Moms In Touch International name be used in conjunction with outside issues.

"Pour out your heart like water before the face of the Lord, lift up your hands toward Him for the lives of your children."
Lamentations 2:19

Guidelines

As you begin:
1. Come as you are.
2. Be faithful in meeting for one hour on a weekly basis. Make this hour a solid commitment to pray.
3. Start and finish on time. If some moms would care to stay longer for fellowship and sharing, do so following the prayer time.
4. Do not serve refreshments. This could be a distraction for your group and an unnecessary burden for the hostess.
5. When meeting in a home, make a decision ahead of time as to how you will handle the phone and doorbell during the meeting. Placing a "Please Do Not Disturb" note on the door and disconnecting the phone might be the answer. This prayer time is precious and should be undisturbed.

Each mom needs:
1. A Bible and notebook for keeping prayer request sheets and other notes. (See sample journal page on Page 11 for recording prayer requests and answers.)
2. Her own Moms In Touch International booklet.
3. To allow another person the privilege of caring for her preschool children during this hour.

In matters of prayer:
1. Pray conversationally in one accord. (See "Praying in One Accord" on Page 12.)
2. Try not to get sidetracked in talking about your requests more than you are praying about them. Share your requests in prayer rather than discussing them first.

3. **EVERYTHING THAT IS SAID OR PRAYED ABOUT IN A MOMS IN TOUCH MEETING IS CONFIDENTIAL.** Nothing said should ever be shared with anyone outside of that Moms In Touch group. Confidentiality cannot be overemphasized.

For the leader:

1. Re-read the Moms In Touch booklet periodically, giving special attention to the guidelines and to the format for prayer time.
2. Pray about everything you do concerning MITI.
3. We strongly suggest that each Moms In Touch group represent only **one** school. This enables you to pray specifically for the needs of that school. College, home school, working mom, and grandparent groups may represent more than one school.
4. For several meetings, you will find it helpful to your group if you spend the first few minutes going over the information on praying in one accord.
5. Don't be alarmed if you do not get through all the prayer topics at each meeting.
6. Follow this format during your prayer hour: praise, confession, thanksgiving, and intercession.
7. Use great care and discretion **not** to impose upon the public school by asking for prayer requests.
8. Once a group is started, it is important to maintain that group for the next school year. As a leader, you should seek to replace yourself if you find you will not be able to continue. It is good to allow another person to lead the group from time to time. This gives you the opportunity to train another person so that the group is not entirely dependent upon you.
9. Summer meetings, if only on a monthly basis, will prove to be a blessing to your group.
10. A personal visit to your school principal is recommended once your group is well established.

Here are some suggested points to cover:

- Acknowledge your appreciation of his/her leadership and the tremendous responsibility that he/she has.
- Share your concern for the pressures that young people are facing today.
- Let him/her know that you belong to a group of moms (called Moms In Touch International) who meet weekly to support the school through prayer.
- Indicate that your group of moms would like to bring treats at different times throughout the year to encourage and show appreciation to the faculty and staff.

Leaders ... We need to know about your group. Please register your group by filling out and returning the order form in the back of this booklet.

Sample Journal Page

Record of Prayer Requests and Answers

Date	Request	Answer	Date

Praying in One Accord

 onversational prayer, or praying in one accord, is the method of praying that is used for our Moms In Touch International groups. One accord praying is agreeing together as directed by the Holy Spirit.

When a group prays in one accord, they concentrate on **one subject at a time**. More than one mom can pray on each subject until that subject is exhausted. It is important not to start a new subject until every aspect of the subject you are praying about is covered. (The leader guides the prayer meeting, although others may introduce a new topic.)

Do not be concerned about silence; God speaks during these times too. Try to keep prayers **short**. This will encourage everyone to participate if the prayers are **simple**.

"When people start praying together in one accord, to our Father in heaven, in the name of Jesus, and practice praying together, things begin to change. Our lives change, our families change, our school, church and communities change. Changes take place not when we study about prayer, not when we talk about it, not even when we memorize beautiful scripture verses on prayer. It is when we actually pray that things begin to happen."*

If you have never prayed conversationally before, please do not feel forced into praying aloud. If you pray silently in your heart, you are still praying in one accord. The more you experience conversational prayer, the easier it will be for you to eventually join in.

By praying in one accord, we hear the heartfelt thoughts of others, and echo those words in our hearts as well. This will cause us to focus on Almighty God and not on ourselves. He will give you the words to say. The eloquence of your prayer is not what is important. **The sincerity of your heart is what God hears.**

*Evelyn Christenson, *What Happens When Women Pray*

Prayer Time

Four Steps of Prayer

P{o} **aise**. Every Moms In Touch prayer session should begin with praise. A beautiful way to praise God is to use Scripture. Our faith becomes strong as we pray back to God His very words.

Let's illustrate the method of praising God in one accord. Choose a passage (Psalm 145:8, for example) and read it aloud. *"The Lord is gracious and full of compassion, slow to anger and abounding in mercy and lovingkindness."*

The group leader might begin by praying, "Oh Lord, you are so gracious. I experience your grace every time I confess sin. You always forgive me. Thank you."

Another mom might continue by praying, "Thank you that your grace is sufficient, especially in those times that I feel so weak and helpless."

Additional prayer on God's grace should continue until that subject is exhausted. If time permits, the leader may introduce the next thought about God, which is His compassion.

As We Praise God:
1. It gives Him the glory.
2. It is declaring, proclaiming, confessing who God is and what He does.
3. It is for our good. It brings freedom and encouragement to our lives because we focus on God and not on the situation.
4. It leads to true stability in life and develops a gentle and quiet spirit.
5. It dispels Satan's power and he leaves. Psalm 22:3, *"God inhabits (resides, dwells in) the praises of His people."*

Here are some suggested Scriptures to use for your adoration and praise time.

Psalm 107:21-22   Psalm 111:1-4
Psalm 28:6-7   Psalm 33:1-12
Psalm 103:1-6   Psalm 36:5-10
Psalm 103:8-13   Psalm 18:1-2
Psalm 145:8-10   Psalm 86:12-13;15
I Chronicles 29:10-12   I Chronicles 16:23-29

onfession. Following your time of praise, God may reveal some areas of your life that are not pleasing to Him. Take a few moments to **silently** confess those sins. Isaiah 59:2 tells us, *"But your iniquities have made a separation between you and your God, and your sins have hid His face from you so that He will not hear."* God says that He will not answer our prayer if there is unconfessed sin. Our relationship must not only be right with Him, but with our fellowman, if we desire Him to hear and answer our prayers.

How do we confess our sin when convicted by the Holy Spirit?
1. Name the sin specifically, agreeing with God that it is sin.
2. Repent concerning the sin. This will result in changed attitudes and actions.
3. Thank God that He has forgiven your sin because of what Christ did on the cross. I John 1:9 (King James): *"If we confess our sins, He is faithful and just to forgive us our sins and to cleanse us from all unrighteousness."*
4. Ask to be filled and controlled by the Holy Spirit. It is a matter of surrendering your will, a total commitment of yourself to God.
   - Command: Ephesians 5:18 (King James): *". . . but be filled with the Holy Spirit."*
   - Promise: I John 5:14-15 (New American Standard): *"And this is the confidence which we have before Him, that, if we ask anything according to His will, He hears us. And if we know that He hears us in whatever we ask, we know that we have the request which we have asked from Him."*

5. By faith, thank Him that He has filled you on the basis of His promise. Do not depend on your feelings. The promise of God's Word, not our feelings, is our authority.

hanksgiving. Another important aspect of a MITI meeting is in giving thanks for how God has answered our prayers. The Apostle Paul exhorts, "*In everything give thanks, for this is the will of God in Christ Jesus concerning you.*" And in Psalm 50:23, God's Word tells us that when we give thanks we honor Him, "*He who offers a sacrifice of thanksgiving honors me.*"

Instead of spending time telling the answer to your prayer, **pray the answer**. The other moms will join in one accord, thanking God with you.

First mom: "Dear Father, thank you that my son has found a Christian friend at school."

Second mom: "Thank you for perfect timing. You knew how lonely he was, and that he needed a Christian friend to help him be strong in You."

Third mom: "We praise You, Father, for Your goodness and that You truly care about every detail of his life."

When one subject is finished, another mom can introduce the next answer to prayer and so on.

Be sure to dedicate this time to thanksgiving only. It will be tempting to mention requests, but remember to focus on giving thanks.

ntercession. During this portion of our prayer time, we come to God, interceding on behalf of our children, teachers, school administrators, and other students. If your group is large, it would be best if you divided the ladies into smaller groups of two or three. The smaller group will allow more time to pray specifically for each child.

Children. Choose a portion of Scripture for your child. As we pray, placing our child's name in that passage, the power of God's Word drives out anxiety and fear and produces faith in us. Remember that faith is taking God at His word and acting accordingly. It is accepting God's words no matter what the circumstances, what the world says, or how we feel.

Here is an example of praying in one accord for our children. Choose a Scripture and read it aloud. For example, Colossians 1:10, *"That you may walk (live and conduct yourselves) in a manner worthy of the Lord, fully pleasing to Him and desiring to please Him in all things, bearing fruit in every good work and steadily growing and increasing in the knowledge of God—with fuller, deeper and clearer insight, acquaintance and recognition."*

The prayer time could go something like this:

First Mom: "Dear Father, I ask that You would help Joe to conduct himself the way a Christian should, no matter how difficult the circumstances."

Second Mom: "Yes, Lord. I ask that Joe would not live one way at home and church and another way at school. I ask that his Christian walk would be part of every aspect of his life."

Third Mom: "And Father, that You would open his eyes to what really pleases You in his conduct."

You may continue praying for Joe on this subject, or be led to other thoughts in the verse. Be sure to exhaust all prayer thoughts for Joe before going on to the next child. Each child is prayed for in the same way.

After you have applied Scripture to your prayers, pray for the specific needs of each child, such as a concern with a teacher, grades, choice of friends, or communication at home. Be sure to record these requests in your notebook.

Prayer Suggestions for our Children.

    1. Pray for their relationship with God:

That they may know *"how wide and long and high and deep the love of Christ is, and know this love that surpasses knowledge."* (Ephesians 3:18,19)

That at an early age they may accept Jesus Christ as their Savior. (II Timothy 3:15)

That they will allow God to work in their lives to accomplish His purpose for them. (Philippians 2:13)

That they will earnestly seek God and love to go to church. (Psalm 63:1, Psalm 122:1)

That they will be caught when guilty. (Numbers 32:23)

2. Pray for godly attributes:

That they will be protected from attitudes of inferiority or superiority. (Genesis 1:27, Philippians 2:3)

That they will respect authority. (I Peter 2:13,14)

That they will be the best students they can be. (Colossians 3:23)

That they will hate sin. (Psalm 97:10)

That they will be able to control their temper. (Ephesians 4:26)

That they will exhibit the fruit of the Spirit in their lives. (Galatians 5:22)

3. Pray for relationships with family:

That they will obey their parents in the Lord. (Proverbs 1:8 and Colossians 3:20)

That they will accept discipline and profit from it. (Proverbs 3:11,12 and 23:13)

That they will love their siblings and not allow rivalry to hinder lifelong positive relationships. (Matthew 5:22, Ephesians 4:32)

4. Pray for relationships with friends:

That they will choose godly friends, who will build them up in the Lord, and be kept from harmful friendships that will lead them astray. (Ecclesiastes 4:10, Proverbs 1:10)

That they will be firm in their convictions and withstand peer pressure. (Ephesians 4:14)

That they will be a friend to the lonely, the discouraged, the lost. (Matthew 25:40, Philippians 2:4)

5. Pray for protection:

From the evil one. (John 17:15)

From drugs, alcohol, and tobacco. (Proverbs 20:1 and 23:31,32)

From victimization and molestation. (Luke 17:1,2)

From premarital sex. (I Corinthians 6:18-20)

From physical danger—accidents and illnesses. (Philippians 4:6)

6. Pray for their future:

That they will be wise in their choice of a mate. Pray now for the one who will marry your child, that he or she will be a Christian and remain pure, and that they will bring one another great joy. (Proverbs 19:14)

That they will be wise in the choice of a career. (Proverbs 3:6)

That they will be wise in the use of their God-given gifts, talents and abilities. (Matthew 25:21)

God deals in miracles. There is nothing too hard for Him— nothing!

I Chronicles 28:9	Ephesians 4:1-2	James 4:8-9	I John 2:15-16
Colossians 1:9-11	Ephesians 4:23-25a	Deuteronomy 10:12-13	I John 3:7
Colossians 2:6-8	Ephesians 4:29	Romans 12:2	I John 1:8-9
Colossians 3:1-2	Philippians 3:10	II Timothy 2:15-16	Matthew 6:33
Ephesians 1:17-19	John 17:26	I Thessalonians 4:3-4, 7	Ephesians 5:1-3

Teachers. As we pray for a teacher, we can be confident that God is hearing and answering our prayers, even though we might not see the results.

It has been shared by many teachers how much they have appreciated and counted on our prayers. One teacher, with tears in her eyes, expressed how she couldn't believe that we would actually take the time and concern to pray for her. She thought that the only other person who ever prayed for her was her mom.

Prayer Suggestions for Teachers:
1. That they will teach with excellence and creativity.
2. That they will use speech that is gracious and pleasant.
3. That they will consider each child as a special individual, not just as "their class" or "their job."
4. That they will have the zeal to make a difference for good in each student's life.
5. That they will not grow weary in well doing, that their commitment to excellence and discipline will not wane.
6. That substitute teachers will be able to control classrooms and be a welcome and positive influence.
7. That those teachers going through difficult personal problems will seek God.

8. That Christian teachers will recognize secular philosophies within the curriculum and openly stand firm in their values.

Scriptures to use in praying for the Christian teacher:

Colossians 1:9-11	Ephesians 4:1-3	Philippians 3:10	II Timothy 2:24-25
Colossians 2:6-8	Ephesians 4:29	Colossians 3:12-15	I John 2:15-16
Ephesians 1:17-19	Ephesians 6:19-20	Colossians 3:17	I John 3:7
Ephesians 3:18-19	Philippians 1:9-11	Colossians 4:3-6	

Prayer Suggestions for Schools:

1. That positions at the state and local level will be filled by men and women with godly principles and values.
2. That new curriculum will be chosen wisely and that it will include biblical standards and high moral values.
3. That each student will learn of God's great love and provision for salvation and accept God's forgiving grace.
4. That children from difficult family situations will receive godly counsel, compassion from their teachers, and make healthy friendships.
5. That your school will be drug and alcohol-free and no addictions will have hold on the youth.
6. That God will protect against unwise choices in dating relationships.
7. That there will be respect for one another, regardless of race or religion.

Prayer Suggestions for Moms In Touch International:

Please take a few minutes to pray for the ministry of Moms In Touch.

1. Pray for other moms to join your group.
2. Pray for each school (by name) in your district to have a MITI group.
3. Pray for a MITI group for every school in your city or immediate area.
4. Pray that every school in your state will have a MITI group.
5. Pray that every nation around the world will have moms praying for their children and schools.
6. Pray the Lord will give the MITI board wisdom and discernment in all decisions they must make on behalf of this ministry.

Words and Deeds

Words and Deeds is an **OPTIONAL** part of Moms in Touch

Ministering Ideas for the School

Personal Ministry. Each mom may take the name of one or more teachers for whom she will be responsible to pray throughout the school year.

- A mom may choose to send a handwritten note similar to the one shown on page 21 to introduce herself.
- Be careful that any notes you write to a public school teacher **do not** carry religious connotations or Scriptures.
- If possible, send a treat periodically with a note of encouragement signed by you.

Group Ministry. Several times throughout the year show appreciation to the entire staff by taking special treats. Be sure to include a card saying "We appreciate you," or something of a similar nature, and signed Moms In Touch International. Pray that these expressions of appreciation might reflect the love of the Lord. Here are some examples of what has been taken to schools:

Muffins, decorated cupcakes, apples and nuts, cookies, basket of candies, sheet cake, donuts, and fruit baskets.

Your Moms In Touch group might plan a dessert, coffee or luncheon in order to express your appreciation in person.

Pray about everything, being sensitive to what might be appropriate for your school.

Instead of taking treats, one elementary MITI group wrote the following Christmas letter. It was so well received that we would like to share it with you.

> *Dear Teachers and Staff of* .... ,
> *With the holiday season upon us, Moms In Touch International wishes each of you a wonderful season of celebration! And we thank you for the gifts you have given to us as mothers.*

In September, we entrusted to you our greatest treasures—our children! Since that time, you have relentlessly and lovingly worked with them.

- You have given them the gift of self-esteem.
- You have given them smiles and approval when they achieved.
- You have given them hugs and understanding when they did not achieve.
- You have disciplined lovingly and fairly and earned their respect.
- You have persevered when our children have sometimes been less than pleasant to work with.
- You have recognized each child as a unique little person. You have striven to help each one begin to reach his or her potential.

Because you care, we know that your work does not always end at 3 p.m. every day. Perhaps you carry many of our little ones home with you occasionally—in your hearts.

So what can we offer you in return during this happy season of giving and receiving?

- We offer you our thanks for loving our children.
- We give you our support and encouragement.
- We offer our time when it is needed.
- We promise to pray for you . . . every week.
- We give you the "honor" of being the greatest elementary school staff anywhere.

Please accept these gifts. They are offered with much love and sincerity!

Moms In Touch International

Sample Letter

Dear ....,

I am a part of a group called Moms In Touch International. We meet once a week to pray for our children and their school. We pray specifically that our children will stand firm in what they believe and that they will make right decisions in difficult circumstances.

I will also be praying for you and your influence at .... school this year. I appreciate your commitment to teaching and pray that you will have wisdom and strength as you carry out your responsibilities this school year.

Sincerely,
(Name)
Moms In Touch International

Praying for the Non-Believer

W hen someone's salvation seems impossible, we need to believe by faith Mark 10:27 "... *with God all things are possible.*" We are in a spiritual battle. But thank God that our spiritual weapons are mighty and our authority in Christ is far above the rulers, powers and forces of darkness. The enemy must yield (II Corinthians 10:3-5). We pray in the name of Jesus, asking for the salvation of students, teachers, and staff members. This takes faith, patience, and persistence. Remember, "...*greater is He that is in you, than he that is in the world.*" (I John 4:4)

Here is an example of one accord praying for the non-believer:

First Mom: "Dear Father, in the name of the Lord Jesus, I pray for the tearing down of all the works of Satan in the life of Pete."

Second Mom: "I pray that his very thoughts will be brought into captivity to the obedience of Christ."

Third Mom: "With the authority of the name of the Lord Jesus, I ask for Pete's deliverance from the power and persuasions of the evil one."

Fourth Mom: "I pray that his conscience will be convicted, and that You, God, will bring him to the point of repentance, and that Pete will listen and believe as he hears or reads the Word of God."

Fifth Mom: "May Your perfect will and purposes be accomplished in and through Pete."

Here are some suggested Scriptures to study and incorporate in your prayer time for non-believers:

John 14:13
II Corinthians 4:3,4
II Peter 3:9
I Peter 1:18,19

II Timothy 2:25,26
I Timothy 2:4-6
Romans 10:13-15
Romans 5:8

Promises to Claim

Matthew 18:19-20 (New American Standard) *"Again I say to you, that if two of you agree on earth concerning anything that they may ask, it shall be done for them by My Father who is in heaven. For where two or three have gathered in My name, there I am in their midst."*

Luke 1:37 *"For with God nothing is ever impossible and no word from God shall be without power or impossible of fulfillment."*

John 14:13,14 *"And I will do—I Myself will grant whatever you may ask in My name (presenting all I Am) so that the Father may be glorified and extolled in (through) the Son. Yes, I will grant—will do for you—whatever you shall ask in My name."*

John 16:24 *"Up to this time, you have not asked a single thing in My name, but now ask and keep on asking and you will receive, so that your joy (gladness, delight) may be full and complete."*

James 1:5-7 (NAS) *"But if any of you lacks wisdom, let him ask of God, who gives to all men generously and without reproach, and it will be given to him. But let him ask in faith without any doubting, for the one who doubts is like the surf of the sea driven and tossed by the wind."*

I John 5:14-15 (NAS) *"And this is the confidence which we have before Him, that if we ask anything according to His will, He hears us. And if we know that He hears us in whatever we ask, we know that we have the requests which we have asked from Him."*

Psalm 84:11 (NAS) *"For the Lord God is a sun and shield; the Lord gives grace and glory; no good thing does He withhold from those who walk uprightly."*

I John 3:21-23 (NAS) *"Beloved, if our heart does not condemn us, we have confidence before God; and whatever we ask we receive from Him, because we keep His commandments and do the things that are pleasing in His sight. And this is His commandment, that we believe in the name of His Son Jesus Christ, and love one another, just as He commanded us."*

Hebrews 10:22,23 (NAS) *"Let us draw near with a sincere heart in full assurance of faith, having our hearts sprinkled clean from an evil conscience and our body washed with pure water . . . for He who promised is faithful."*

Luke 11:13 (NAS) *"If you then, being evil know how to give good gifts to your children, how much more shall your Heavenly Father give the Holy Spirit to those who ask Him?"*

Jeremiah 33:3 (NAS) *"Call to Me, and I will answer you, and I will tell you great and mighty things, which you do not know."*

John 15:7 *"If you live in Me—abide vitally united to Me—and My words remain in you and continue to live in your hearts, ask whatever you will and it shall be done for you."*

Matthew 21:22 *"And whatever you ask for in prayer, having faith and believing, you will receive."*

In Touch With You, Lord

Theme Song: Moms In Touch International

Words & Music by Connie Kennemer

Edition: 4/30/94

Statement of Faith

1. We believe the Bible to be the inspired, the only infallible authoritative Word of God.
2. We believe that there is one God, eternally existent in three persons: Father, Son, and Holy Spirit.
3. We believe in the deity of our Lord Jesus Christ, in His virgin birth, in His sinless life, in His miracles, in His vicarious and atoning death through His shed blood, in His bodily resurrection, in His ascension to the right hand of the Father, and in His personal return in power and in glory.
4. We believe that for the salvation of a lost and sinful person regeneration by the Holy Spirit is absolutely essential.
5. We believe in the present ministry of the Holy Spirit, by whose indwelling the Christian is enabled to live a godly life.
6. We believe in the resurrection of both the saved and the lost; the saved unto the resurrection of life and the lost unto the resurrection of damnation.
7. We believe in the spiritual unity of believers in our Lord Jesus Christ.
8. We believe God concerns Himself mercifully in the affairs of men, and that He hears and answers prayer.

ORDER FORM
To Insure Proper Processing
Please Print and Fill Out Completely

Name _____

Address _____

City _____

State/Province _____ Zip/Postal Code _____

Country _____Phone (_____) _____

    I'm a group leader ☐   I'm a group member ☐   I'm interested in starting a group ☐

    I would like to receive your newsletter ☐

School _____

    College ☐   High School ☐   Intermediate ☐ Elementary ☐   Home School ☐

Comments _____

_____

BOOKS		QUANTITY	AMOUNT
English	**$5.00 each**		$
Spanish	**$2.50 each**		$
Braille	**$5.00 each**		$
BROCHURES			
English	**No charge**		$
Spanish	**No charge**		$

Books also available in Anglican, Arabic,
Chinese, German, Romanian,
Russian, and Swahili.

	AMOUNT
SubTotal	$
10% Optional First Class Shipping within the U.S.	$
25% Optional Overseas Airmail	$
Gift to Moms In Touch International (*U.S. Tax Deductible*)	$
TOTAL AMOUNT (Please do not send cash)	$

✓ All amounts shown are suggested donations,
postpaid, U.S. Currency.

✓ Books and Brochures are sent Third Class Mail.

✓ Expect 3-4 weeks for delivery unless First Class
postage is included.

✓ Overseas orders should be paid with an
International Money Order or personal check
payable in U.S. Funds.

✓ Make checks or money orders payable to
Moms In Touch International.

Mail To
**MOMS IN TOUCH
INTERNATIONAL**
P.O. Box 1120
Poway, CA 92074-1120, USA

ORDER FORM

To Insure Proper Processing
Please Print and Fill Out Completely

Name _____

Address _____

City _____

State/Province _____ Zip/Postal Code _____

Country _____Phone (_____) _____

I'm a group leader ☐   I'm a group member ☐   I'm interested in starting a group ☐

I would like to receive your newsletter ☐

School _____

College ☐   High School ☐   Intermediate ☐   Elementary ☐   Home School ☐

Comments _____

BOOKS		QUANTITY	AMOUNT
English	$5.00 each		$
Spanish	$2.50 each		$
Braille	$5.00 each		$
BROCHURES			
English	No charge		$
Spanish	No charge		$

Books also available in Anglican, Arabic,
Chinese, German, Romanian,
Russian, and Swahili.

SubTotal	$
10% Optional First Class Shipping within the U.S.	$
25% Optional Overseas Airmail	$
Gift to Moms In Touch International *(U.S. Tax Deductible)*	$
TOTAL AMOUNT (Please do not send cash)	$

✓ All amounts shown are suggested donations,
   postpaid, U.S. Currency.

✓ Books and Brochures are sent Third Class Mail.

✓ Expect 3-4 weeks for delivery unless First Class
   postage is included.

✓ Overseas orders should be paid with an
   International Money Order or personal check
   payable in U.S. Funds.

✓ Make checks or money orders payable to
   Moms In Touch International.

Mail To
**MOMS IN TOUCH
INTERNATIONAL**
P.O. Box 1120
Poway, CA 92074-1120, USA